THE ETERNAL SEASON AND THE AGE OF LIGHT

poems by joel anthony ciaccio

Rad Press Publishing

Raised in rural Pennsylvania, **joel anthony ciaccio** published his first book of poetry in the summer of 2021 at the age of thirty-eight. He is the author of one collection of poetry—you're holding it.

THE ETERNAL SEASON
AND THE AGE OF LIGHT

poems by joel anthony ciaccio

Rad Press Publishing

Copyright © 2021 by joel anthony ciaccio
ISBN: 9780578901343
First Edition
For more information about the author visit thejacpoet.com

radpublishing.co

Table of contents:

THE ETERNAL SEASON
AND THE AGE OF LIGHT

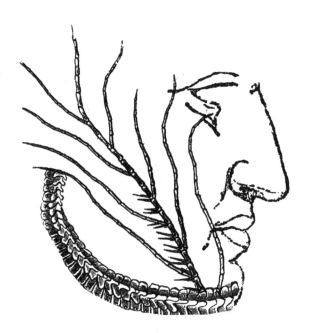

The Indivisible Subdivision

What are the subdivisions of life?
This moment is marveling at trees
and their prodigious branching.
Making myself a student of this teacher,
I call it by name, not knowing its language.

The unseen movements
are mirrored in our respective reaches.
At the edges, our forms are familiar
with the paths of growing.
Boasting no predictable patterns,
the ways in which we grow are somehow known
to the tree and me before the forms appear.

Does man and his forms, this moment,
forever flower forward?

Like hearing the echo before the scream,
or seeing ripples before throwing stones;
the tree and me both scream our graspless reach
through the void of formless life:
echoing ripples from similar throes.

Like light moving through the black,
life pushes back
against the distant dark approaching.

In integration, the play of this
becomes an interaction yielding
infinite iterations . . .

from mountains to man,
from cosmos to clan,
this frequency band
tethers titans to sand;
and threatens to stand
in defiance of man's
reliance on land.
It shifts on time's sand,
is granular to grand,
the constituent in blend,
and bland as bleeding
the blood's relation to
the seed of love;

wrenched from reach,
and cleave and tug.
This is tagged and stamped,
is pulsed in the blood.
This is ground to earth
and birth giving birth.
This is the oldest light
touching earth
in repetitions rehearsed.

This is nothing ventured,
nothing spared.
This is every follicle
of creature's hair.
The breadth of breath,
and conceit of mind,
is miraculous memory,
and time entwined.
Is mundane and divine
and relative in kind.
Kindred to pine
and poplar,
like people
and purpose.

Listen, now—hush, now—be still.
Swell, now—pulse, now—be moved.
Rush, now—swell, hush—be true.

(Eye can't un-see.
Ear can't un-hear.
What man has married,
his mind reflects it.)

Listen!
The hymnotic throng
of that eternal song
hung in human ears
echoes in words familiar as sight.

This is the sound of everything at once.
This is the sight that saturates senses:
the movement of the formless taking shape
is life undivided.

~ questions ~

Into the Fog Swell

Into the fog swell my traveler!
Be certain of your form in formless voids.
Hold your colors close cloudy trespasser!
Lay claim to the ground where roots reach for vein.
    Into another shape of light.
    Another shade of shine.

Set your voice secure my sentinel,
prepare for friendless echoes as you scream.
Project your radiating sentience
forcing a field on an opaque scrim.
    Set secure the tap of presence.
    Secure the tone's timbre.

Wander at whim where you will—step strong!
Blindly anchor footholds on earthen braille,
reading language on ground and graveled strip,
recalling all the ghosts that made you brave.
    Wander freely lapsing device.
    Freely listen and list.

Graded ground and faded hue now blend,
senses sustain a droning stimulus
magnifying the beat of pulsing blood,
betraying your mortal stamina.
    Graded ground your feet can handle.
    Ground that is flat you fear.

Into the fog swell my traveler!
There are colors waiting to kiss your eyes,
there are sounds your ears will gladly tremble.
Somewhere deep down you feel this dawning rise.
    Into another mode of time.
    Another mist of man.

Human Projectors I

There is a light inside every wick
before a candle ever burns. Even
if you never hazard starting
the sulfur countdown to blackened
fingertips, know that the wince
of your eyes accounts for each
potential flame. Whether in
focusing or the anticipation of pain,
the reason's rate becomes
animated before the extinguishing
occurs. And knowing this only half
explains how bulbs can consume a
similar fire before any current can
flow to filament. So too, the one track
mind, grounded in graphs and
grids, allows patterns to flower
forward unhindered. Blossoming
the spiral architecture that implies
design in the miraculous mind, but just
prior to binding belief in binary creeds.

In the Same Way That Trees Bend

In the same way that trees bend, I submit.
    Their bark taunts my skin to scab,
    my callous nature remits
to wear experience implying age,
    to texture growth in plain sight;
    demanding that I feel it.

In the same way that trees bend, I am staid.
    Branches bound by sap's speed speak,
    sinew echoes bone's blood-cry,
roots reach unseen ground fed by life's decay,
    leaves lose color, forfeit shade;
    death's pang dirges underfoot.

In the same way that trees bend, we both breathe.
    Whether wind makes forests scream,
    how I, at hearing, gasp awe
at laughter mocking mutual exchange
    inhale to exhale we match,
    making spiritus vitae.

In the same way that trees bend, we resist.
    Woods deprive eyes an Eden,
    I deny ties that ground me.
Alone together, vulnerably tethered,
    perfect stillness our standing;
    companion captives and free.

This is why I bend with trees.

Prey, Unprepared

I was unprepared for moments like these.
Felt a feeling, deep down some may miscall
    sadness.

(I ignored it)

How foolish I, to fear tears
    of instinct
in open fields of reverie,

when wind could mean lions waiting,
ready to run the savanna
    for food.

Unprepared, I brave these miraculous
    plains knowing that,

once exposed, lost memories
rarely escape the hunger of
    healing.

Past Life I - Déjà vu

If I was a bird, I don't recall treading light like water.
I don't recall the kind of feather I followed,
or creed swallowed that made me
race the earth's rotation
in a double helix dance
over the almost and already dead.
But this reminds me of how my forms
are reconciled among the clouds.
We know not north from south,
yet carry on without compass, all the same.
How many flocks does my DNA contain?
How many birds turn the churning machinery
of decay inside my cells like clocks?
And when time runs out,
knows how to flee from frost by flying south
to another north.

Range Round and Through a Blanker Page

Range round and through a blanker page
that margins consume, and frightens to flight
    the hand's heated blood.
Blankly callous of potential, a cold
shadow grips and chills the youthful summer
    from my in-folded forms.
And this emptiness is written in the finger's print
    like a lettered threat;
as with touch, the light's promise fall's short.

Range round and through a darker day
whose graying skies dim a lighted hue,
and despair to dance
    the flame's flickering blade.
Darkly wanton of praise, an extinguished
passion moves the autumnal soul
toward the churning machinery of decay,
    anticipating frost.
And this gloom looks for space to gain
    unto my absent eyes;
as with retinal sight, the spirits' fire is inverted.

Press on and grip the passing phase
that comes in seasons and senses sustain
    the mind's memorial scent.
Progressively accepting of age,
a forgotten fever consumes my wintry days,
swelling the reach of dawn's recession.
And this chill numbs the fear whose stench
    is spared the nose;
as sweeter smells, the prick of thorns protect.

Abide and thrive in ancient rhythms
whose patterns sequence time and refrains repeat
    the soul's sympathetic chant.
Ancestrally tethered of kind, a soundless song
heralds the spring's morning,
turning my solar lilt toward warmer light.
And this thaw rouses the throng of that eternal song
    hung in my ears;
as with hearing, the universal drone is hymnotic.

Range round and through the coming fray
that welcomes you back and never negates
      the past's present taste.
Calmly suggestive of bent,
a distaste for the temporary reveals eternity's
ever-changing face and immutable ways.
And this is a forever that frames the illusion of days,
      taxing the tongue's palate;
as with taste, the limit of flavor is a closed mouth.

And this is the silence that covers your mettled way
      forward, towards the insatiable grave;
as with being, the blank page expands.

L'entre Deux "Everythings"

This middling world is all we know.
It's neither too fast nor too slow.
To me it seems that we compress reality, don't we?
How wonderful then that every single "everything"
makes room for more mystery.

More space to spend time in,
more ground to gain,
more places to put Adam and Eve in,
when needing modern clothes.

When, really, all we need to know
is there is nothing faster than now
and no thing slower than what is not.

Look! see how the trees have hurried
to grow bespoke leaves
and cast a sense of shade
with stunning precision

before us.

At this very moment, you have outrun
billions of stars in their courses
with the slightest movements.

All the atoms in an inch of bone
bear the atmospheric load
as much as any stone;

yet you feed it to the capillaries
of your lungs
as fairly as any mother bird
to her young.

The point is this: when weighing
what to do, give yourself a break because
you've likely got a lot going on,

and, really, you are fine
precisely
where you are.

Pulse

Happen I to chance upon a point of pulse. . .

. . . on a body aged in memory.
Haunted by clocks keeping time and secrets
subdivided in the subtle language
of the heart's irregular rate and pattern.

It's not as simple as. . .

 . . .contraction and expansion.
   Active and resting,
    surge and interval
   (counting, counting).

Lucky me—

—to see this silent flickering.
This sanguine metronomic throb.

To spot a sign of life lingering
so close to the surface,
and so delicately vulnerable
that calloused fingers feel nothing.

So do I long for a gentle check-in,
a knowing smile of understanding,
an agile mind of recollection and presence,
and a heart of all steadiness and acuity.

Hidden in plain sight.
Finger on the pulse.

Privilege

I
I wonder if
early man
before his higher
senses still

stepped lightly on
when looking
up under distant
show of stars

not knowing proofs
by subtle
shifts as common as
can consume

he moving toward
his dawning
rise as city lights
dim the view

II
a modern man
in all his
ways wore thin the threads
clothed in age

aided by clocks
looks backward
past his present self
forward walks

the show of brains
blinding sight
when frontal thoughts think
time like food

a spinning feast
in which he
slept gluts minds though peace
milds his moods

III
feels like
privileged excess
holding
the human race

hostage
to time(s) when time's
seen in
in greater steps

guiding
reason's sure tide
that one
consistently

faces
while other times
fail(ed) to
blend(s) darker hues

. . . how privileged that hallowed height.

Primordial

Privately, I concede that
My mind is still on the savanna.
   Even when walking an avenue and
    All roads run the grids that make us great,
the mind recognizes artifice, and
Primes ancient gears. Or, at least, Deals a dose of doubt.

Order be damned when modern minds
Deliberately assert that man's ascent is
    Primary to purpose. driven by life
    Events, being is formed by tidal nights'
Allowance, lapping the generational
pageant playing out in our DNA.

        ulterior to miraculous motives,
        minds emerge as dominant threats,
        thwarting the lions of superstition.
        keeping the cortisol lying in wait,
        pools the oasis of a hallowed unknown,
        hidden in anxious tall grass or mirage.

Pray, I'm More Ideal than
My knuckle-dragging past.
   for fear frightens to flight the
   hand's heat when
Ordinary ghosts, expressed in genes,
Dial back the sun to shine on quickening blood.

i fear i have

i fear i have nothing to say.

as the trees stand and the soil speaks
    home and slow harm,
my folded forms know this knowledge
    gnaws at footfall.

the circular promise
    to be taken up the trunk,
        softens my calloused intellect,

prepares my flesh for the leaves' journey;
a natural irony lost in speech.

i fear i have nothing to feel.

as worlds turn, rounding right angles,
    bends and buoys
best laid plans, twists and braids bramble
    among senses;

time tatters and tears my
    mumbled praying with life's salt.
        setting the arrowed hands forward

towards an unknown, star-bent freedom call
leading me home, though i am lost in touch.

i fear i have nothing to see.

as the light is lensed in transit,
    before landing,
it bends towards me. turning on land,
    favoring ground

over night's black faces.
    turning toward day to ward off
        distant out-of-focus places.

capturing my dust mote's pale blue drift,
while others linger and lilt lost in sight.

i feel i have nothing to fear.

a single star, fair in sighting,
    north by nothing,
hoping to grasp signs in seeing,
    blind as bleeding,

guides my single vision.
    steadfast as a tree bears fruit,
        staid roots mirror moon's lunar lock

to tidal shifts on shoreless reason,
while the sea's sons send maydays to the gods.

. . . .

o uncertain point of light
guide my fixed human eye!
frost and keats can keep their eremite!
i just ask thee make my crooked forms straight.

Pole that pulls at
    Air that covers the
        Hiss of breathing creatures.

paths of being i may forward through walk.
blossoms of moment's many-faced fruitings.
from ground to darkest skies with empty hands
    i pray:
        i fear
            i have.

Neither Shall You Fear the Dark I

Neither shall you fear the dark approaching,
its measured advance, devouring time;
nor dusk's faded hold on day's retreating.
Gird your senses against time's taught tenure,
ground yourself in the infinite dancing,
wane to this perennial partner's wax.

Instead, cherish this spinning moment,
burn with the heart,
cast your colors on shadows,
x-ray their one-dimensioned forms.

Exhaust your pulsing reach with dawning rise
and lay lithely in moistened fields!
Christened slick touch of woman's unfolding:
    two lovers in-folded,
    form within form.

Marrowing pulsed carnal asymmetry,
dances like dark does on bright days.
Now bone's blood-cry comes from an other heart.
    An other source,
    differing in color.

Recoiling from life's throe in distant dark;
two, reeling, take torch to another chest,
imparting fire to another's heart.
The unseen spinning moment will not rest,
forever flowering this flame forward,
proclaiming: neither shall you fear the dark.

The Eternal Season

The eternal season
is one season
of shifting face
and sleight of hand:

a celestial kaleidoscope
dropped among the dusty heavens.

A needle drops—

Listen! humanity's song
is playing in the black.

Sing love,
    sing war,
        sing cultures and kingdoms!
Sing art,
    sing eras,
        sing generations and seasons!

The eternal season
is one season!
One face, ever-changing.
One moment, forever spinning.
One perfect stillness standing.

And for me, standing still as I am
(wholly human with a penchant for meaning),
only secures my foolish understanding
of a world that can never be held in place,
but always allows me to try.

Still Moved True

Still as I am,
am I as still as I ought?
Ought I (as still as I am)
when captive to time's arrowed heart,
    move?

Moved as I am,
am I as moved as I think?
Think I (as moved as I am)
forever in a moment's blink,
    true?

True as I am,
am I as true as I seem?
Seem I (as true as I am)
a traveler caught in between,
    still?

Stillness of being
is being at a place in life
when you can claim the clamor of years that add up;
a collection of moments you didn't know were accumulating.
Memories waiting patiently for an evaluation
that results in the formation of your future—
or at least your movement forward—
and a view of the past that seems permanent
    but is relative to experience.

All experience
is past experience—even
that which you perceive to be present.
The most recent moments are only more readily
available, because they are woven seamlessly into
the vortex of the present, but are no less past. And what
you consider to be the past—the deep past—does not exist;
at least not in its current recollected form.

This is how one travels in time:
by the acquisition of memory.
A conjuring trick that can only occur now,
    and never anywhere else.
This stills the miraculous mind into a kind of contemplative stupor
from which movement may be borne.

Movement of the mind
is the mindful manipulation of memory,
where the practice and method of extracting

lessons becomes a constant preoccupation. Not a distraction
to pass the time, but a distraction from time. The illusion
of control with events that have already happened,
or have not yet happened, or perhaps will never happen.
And not just the control of mere circumstance,
     but of other people too.

Other people who
are likely doing the same thing as you
with their mind's movement. The main difference
is that you do not play as big a role in their mind as you think.
To them you are a constituent and insignificant ingredient.
You are, at least, granular to their experience and, at most,
a supporting role in their hidden drama.

And the only sign of this that you will ever get to see
is when a catatonic gaze clears the way for
projections in the periphery, leaking an interior cinematic language
needing a screen to direct its aperture towards,
though closing its doors just before any words
     betray the projector by tears.
This is calculated to appear as accidental—
so that it remains untranslated, never written down,
and may as well be a dead language—
     but is understood by nearly everyone.
It is the only outward sign of the internal drama
within every passing personal genre on a crowded street.

And so each mind is a miraculous venue,
a grand private stage with a singularly transfixed audience.
All blurring the focus of life simultaneously
     by blending truth with plausibility.

Truth in thought
is thinking through what is thought to be true.
What has been unquestioned by eons of generations—
in defiance of the infinity of numbers—the sum total
of which generates a palpable sense of fear and trembling
     at the throne of the unknown,
and is elevated and ordained by the revering
of what cannot possibly be known;
only interacted with, through a prostrated existence:
a prone pitiful posturing our penchant obsession
     with meaning makes us.
Mattering not more than merely mapping out
the farther edges of our minds.
Minds mired in matter and prone to reach
for that which is beyond reproach.

     You see...

minds reach and matter grasps,
time keeps and eternity lasts

...provided there is still enough time.

So we graph our lives
on lines of time,
to teach our reach
how far is far
and how long is long.

And in doing so,
we gird ourselves
in grid and ground,
with hopes of grasp
that leaves the grass
to launch our lives
beyond the point
of arrowed time.

Still, there is movement in truth.

A hushed reduction
towards a waiting absurdity.
The abolition of arrival
summons a kind of vertigo
in the thinking mind
of the thinking man
    (as in humanity).
Meanwhile, life pulls us towards
the heart of all there is:
a nexus network of
nerve endings firing in the dark,
in denial of neuropathy.
In defiance of synapse gaps
of gods and destroyers of maps
passed down, passed on
by miraculous minds.
Distilling life down to
the indivisible subdivision,
the perfect moment,
the life of elusive light—
join me in the lonely voyeurism!

A place where and when and how
I am
still moved true.

~ answers ~

Man, Meaning, and the gods

Ponders a puddle through reflection:

> *"Happen I to chance upon a place so*
> *perfect!"*

prays the puddle.

> *"The dimensions must have been precisely*
> *measured!"*

(This is...)

How shallow man's muddy waters
shape the ignorance of other oceans.

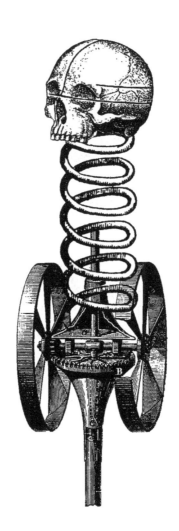

Human Projectors II

There are many images in the mind
before light's shine ever shows shape.
Even if your preference for composition
differs from your vernacular wake,
understand that these things fold the
forms before being placed in frames.
And how this helps to capture meaning
in human terms when it concerns the
stories that survive their travel through
time. We pass these inventions on from
mind to mind, only ever resting captive on
the tip of each and every tongue, like
tungsten waiting to glow. Oh how we
shudder the frame rates that tell these
stories slow! All so we can claim the calm
before a coming storm as our own
and how we name now knowing it is never
gone. When, really, this can only occur
in the moment just prior to
language leaving the lens at lifespeed.

Bones Cry Blood

What is the bone's blood-cry?

> All bones cry different blood.
From iron's dark marrow—waiting in calcium—
the skeletal prison frames the in-folded forms,
unleashes long lessons' slow-flowing agency,
to pool at proud tongue's tip, and speak single colors
> one at a time.

Bone's blood-cry bleeds colors within life's graded hue.
Regardless of sense, the knowing members hear it.
Not the sound of ears, but of eras' lapping tide.
Hear the perfect moment sizzle reason's salt-sense
on razor-edged safe shores' emerging consciousness,
> standing stranded.

Eyes that envy breaking tides, chase urgent visions,
levy rushing currents. Directing channeled sight
with widening aperture towards narrowing scenes,
things unseen—unsensed—are perceived in obliqueness,
coaxing sounds that soon name a claimed periphery
> eyes can't unsee.

A watchtower stands uncertain on favored ground,
for future souls from the southern cradle's palace
to shrug off the steady work of waiting for christ
the child to come from a sepulcher of man's make.
Cry bone's blood, falling tower! Cast ivory pearls—
> thick, warm, and wet!

Seeds explode slowly over turning rocks in time's
archaic gravity clockwork menagerie.
Like the descending sun stretches shadows daylong,
so do seeds to soil concede faith in future light.
Each reaches out to each, by rising like the trees
> that bend in time.

A Distillation of All There Is

Life has its searching ways
that probe mind and marrow.
A peering, eyeless gaze,
unblinking in permanence.

And ravished as I am
any day of the week
by this unquenchable,
thirsting swallow—

I am reminded of this:

that I am a permeable substance,
vulnerable to gulp and consumption,
diffuse and spread thin,
a beggar's economy
at the tablecloth's fringe,
a granular constituent of other's
        projections from within.

And without surgical
        precision,
but in casted wide nets
        I surrender.
        I submit.

I am the dissolve in life's
        solvent.
The disintegrate amongst
a perforated sift.

A distillation of all there is.

Past Life II - Amnesia
(for Alfonse & Timothy)

If I was a storm,
I don't remember the land that
made me weep my floating weight.

I don't remember the shape
of my terrible sounds—the wrath of god
on the ground—

falling on all the ears
there to hear;
and kept

in every place inaccessible
to the malleable
conveyance of memory.

In shapes
no mouth
can make
to speak,

in words
no brain
can bend
to will;

the shift
of hue
told on
a hill,

and the story of how a stone moved an inch,

is in all the ground that pulled
my vaporous past along.
Its passing was transcribed in patterns
of matter no mind can now apprehend.

No math can chart a heart's
progress over time (though we try).
Whether it softens or hardens says
little of love and less of life.

The inverse relationship
of that clenched fist
to it's every irregular egress,

beating out one more moment
of life's Morse code;
releasing all the bloody
thunder that made me

is what I remember.

Waits for the Wind

I listen to the wind outside
    from within my truck,
and wonder at the treetops,
    and how it must feel

to be that far from its rooted trunk;
    and how
(having fewer rings
    to show for its years),
this notion makes its higher movements
    a most thrilling sight!

Tender branch, tender branch
where would I break by weaker force?
I am merely a slower wind
    walking by.
Mostly made of your future food.
Hundreds of me equal so few of you.

Yet each time I see your winsome wave
    above
(that inverted root drinking the sun's soil
and wind's wild trellis!),

my inner child descends the tree
    in adult caution,
because it breaks falls from lower branches,
mirrors the years your heights have reached my roots,
and waits for the wind to pass.

The Lions (Inside)

It's easy to think we're like lions
who rest most of the day
on the savannas of our pride.
Who assume we will be those who survive,
and for whom everything in sight was made.

When, really, those who'd speak of an other side
    have already died;
leaving alive those behind to speak wholly
    on their behalf.

It's easy to take real lions
that tore flesh and broke bones
    to restore their own,

seriously.

Easier still, to put pulpit words in the mouth
    of a dead man
than to let the lion-hunger from inside his
    savanna mind

through the terror of his teeth.

Passed life, no one speaks
    of this.

We Are The Machines of Meaning

We are the machines of meaning.
Matter geared and mired
masters of hidden processes,
gnawing secret knowledge
signatures in the material night.

Alchemists of allegory
exacting toll and toil
scream the void to gain dawning light.
Now language walks upright,
outpacing the gears of understanding.

Make blood lose its color and taste,
nourish love of life used,
spend the marrow and breach the lung—
hazard iron its hue—
gasp the waking pageant wrought in the fray.

In-folded forms blossom with age.
Timing despairs the dance
that meaning's light never negates.
Movement grips fixity
and speaks beauty like a nameless flower.

Still, wholly human, I stand still.
Seasons will wax and wane.
Tides will shift on shoreless reason,
sifting precious knowing,
elapsed in minds tethered to time's arrow.

Here's to Heroes
(for Louis CK, among others)

I

Here's to heroes as they fall
    short or long in the mind's length:
    edge-graphed to grids of greatness,
    brought to ledge with white knuckle—
    pale palm, burning friction red.

Their favor stands uncertain.
    As on high, they are brought low.
    Falling all, failing forfeit
    in irregular seasons.
    En masse to more massive tides.

II

There rises humanity
    on dislocated shoulders,
    probing the empty sockets,
    scavenging the evidence,
    erasing soul's signatures.

There rises humanity's
    boiling scream at kettle's black.
    Brimming, bursting, burning out!
    Spent the candle's wick and wax,
    flame the shade of shadow's doubt.

III

Our heroes were useful once;
    one time, when timing was right.
    When up the charge swells the fight,
    flown high false-flag virtue signs.
    Fought fierce history's hindsight.

Once an ally, context now
    drowns in human's white-noise wave.
    Nuance dies in outrage, while
    sin's tax-exempt class controls
    culture's sole, fickle conscience.

IV

Fair faded in feigning fair—
    keep strong that Heaven's Gate Stare!
    Those public, secret handshakes
    that move goalposts on allies
    opining—you eunuch pawns!

Meanwhile, cast to curtain call
    shows all their pride, never faults.
    History's rite, side-worship
    bacchanal: human heroes
    are all fare in rise and fall.

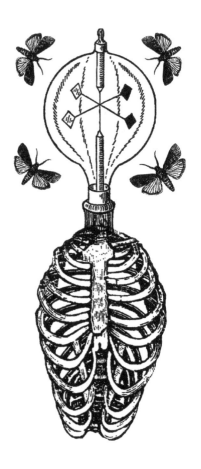

Broken Barns

It's the broken barns in those lonely fields
    that break my heart.
This pedestal of nature showcases
    human folly,
        reflects our common journey towards repose,
        and the familiar comfort of being placed.
Those lonely barns sing my soul in light's lap
    with photon's fragile frame.
        Crossing our paths along sun-guided tides,
        expressing in texture
the uniform of life's languid desire,
    here in this well-worn field.

How slight the sun shifts over cracked paint peels'
    creeping age crawl!
We both walk the ways of spinning houses
    with tactile grace
        on curling forms of the heart's higher sense.
        Coaxing bone's splinter-currents up the soul,
the handless time of faceless clock-shapes
    master hidden processes,
        that mimic stillness and the twice-told tale
        of miraculous minds
(passed down, passed on), and how we travel time
    to tell the sun its age.

There is an elegy here to behold—
    not heard or held.
Life moves in moments down the salted ground
    towards waiting tears,
        bound in primordial weeping exile.
        Waiting patiently, roots tap nitric needs
carrying the circular promise up
    the matter that makes us
        host and hostage to chemical matters.
        Under the sky's saltless drift,
the friction floods all there is and grounds and
    drowns the sun down in soil.

My feet know I walk this ship's carbon plank,
    tree's future fuel,
for you to know that I am barn-broken
    borrowed kindling.
        A flower walking forward, mortal flame,
        frame for a name, wick in candle's waxed time.

Graphing pastoral decay on the ground's grid,
    I walk articulate
        a long green acre mile to watch the barn's
            faded-color swan song.
This side of life's graded hue welcomes rust and
    wakes sand in broken glass.

Like life's blood, light bleeds patterns blessing sense
    with instant food.
The lymphatic wind blows the stirring scene
    with sequin sounds.
        Shimmers and shines my heart-broken body.
        Galvanizing the barn's blood with light, life's
matte reflection of synapses' crabbing
    through vein and windowpane,
        drumming the webbed light with wind-woven thread
            in arachnid pleasure,
finds me here now! How apt that my heart's fire
    burns barn-bright in this field.

Do Not Give Your Power Away

Do not give your power away.
There is nothing to gain from the slow drip
transfusion of unfolded forms.
Do not give your power away.
Make of marrow's threat a fearsome promise
    to rust death its iron.

Spend your power in human ink.
Empty yourself and swell your pulsing reach.
Gain the ground nourished by compost
rushing downward at decay's speed.
Man, leaves, bone, and branch beneath sodden steps,
    slightly sink in the grave.

Write as if the words don't matter.
Wrestle with wording and definition.
Change unchanging sounds in syntax,
unleashing letters from their bonds,
and the words will submit, bending in form,
    free from mute, man-made gods.

Speak! Scream the void of formless life
and shape infinity in finite forms.
Dark and light should tremble alike,
making myth yield to graded hue.
The palette will bleed towards opacity,
    shaping human white noise.

Do not give your power away.
Deny belief its tempting proposal.
Functional, at best, it lingers.
Corrosive, at worst, it remains.
Outsourced meaning offers nothing to gain—
    don't give power away.

Neither Shall You Fear the Dark II

Neither shall you resist dark's recession,
its eager retreat at time's entreaty,
nor dawn's hued alchemical obsession.
Give over love of controlling time's tense,
grant yourself in favored abolition
from many seasons to one unique form.

Instead, relish the transformation,
lead with the heart,
own your colors and shadows,
embrace their integrated forms.

Immerse your pulsing reach within the fray,
marry minds to the eternal,
tether time's arrow to uncertainty:
    betrothed of beloved,
      spouse and espoused.

Corporeal node of human frequency,
singing like songs do on taut strings.
Now drone's throng hangs on no thing of substance,
    no thing of flesh—bereft
    and wrought of reach.

Resounding with life's howl in current caul;
you, feeling, fear nothing of consequence,
nurturing nature in nothing's soul.
The unheard universal song's absence
forever fills a skeptic's fancies and
neither fears nor resists darkness' call.

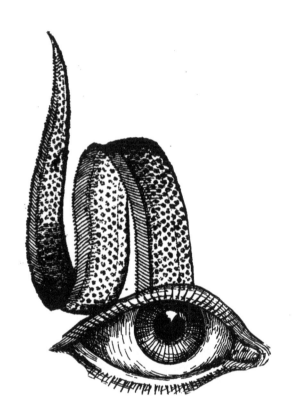

Sometimes Life Falls On Me

I

Sometimes life falls on me like sight for eye's sake.
That prying moment when vision's prayer
    wrenches my lids open
in supplication before awe's altar,
propitiating the blind moment's blink,
crushing kingdoms whole in their pride.

The defiant scenes are captured in seeing
black silhouettes on tree-covered hilltops.
    At sepia sunset,
a cast ombré sky caps the dome above,
pulling my dead-star-forged carbon coil towards
twilight, tracing my backlit forms.

Spread out and bloodless in fragile array,
strewn on land and sky, sewn at unseen seam
    of horizon's retreat,
my vision's folded in at close of day—
written in nature's tattered dereliction—
finding rest among the relics.

II

Sometimes life comes to me like sound before ears.
Before hearing captures minds in man's speech.
   Thoughtful before thinking—
uttered in a hush of fear and trembling—
a rapture of madness disguised as faith
speaks its peaceful, godless order

in frequencies common to the soul's stirring,
as unseen movements paint my mind's matter
   a shade of gray music.
Quantized to this subtle rate and pattern,
the heart's irregular language will speak
meaning's flame to life's kindling time.

My aural sense is aroused in attention
to this stirring sea-tide blown wind without.
   Storming my forms within,
the Trojan metaphors are most welcomed,
while the white noise works on other senses
that follow the head and the heart.

III

Sometimes life is not the blind Braille guiding touch,
but the mindless Morse code of a heartbeat
	found in a pulsing path.
There are rocks to be read by hands and feet
of weather patterns our pebble-planet's
orbit grinds down to time's fine sand.

No touch can catch a tree's growth from seed to flame
like smoke! Releasing shapes that warn flowers
	how their carbon can burn
before sulfur's smell settles in their cells;
fermenting knowledge in sentient guts,
ending worlds in methane whimpers.

Follow the flower that needs no knowledge to grow
and what waters its roots will quench your calm.
	Breathe in this fog swell's cloud
and make a mist of man that mocks water.
Drench your sight in the alchemy of sense,
where life falls golden in the soul.

The Age of Light

They say that
the oldest light in the universe
is proof of our beginning.

They say that
these ancient rays have traveled far,
not from a star,
but from chaos.
And have now settled down, sitting
in the rocking chair background
    of our skies
and darken and fade,
and rock and sway,
watching all the eight-minute old
rays run and dance and play.

    "What a marvelous display!"
says this old light.

    "You'll come sit beside us sometime.
    Not now, but some day or some night."

They say that
light does not age by slowing down,
but by diffusing and spreading out.
Their wrinkles are worn
in stretched-out wavelengths
living in the loneliest places of the cosmos,
waiting patiently for visitors.

This old light says,
    "You'll come too".

They say that
we are the stuff of stars,
that we are the light and the life
and the way out of death.
Rising from the aftermath
of a galactic controlled burn—
ashes to ashes and dust to dust
    we will return!

They say that
in this moment
we are a universe concerned . . .

                                    . . .with matter,
                                    with meaning,
                                    with eyes perceiving
                                    particulate ends
                                    and-or beginnings.
                                    Cosmic horizons
                                    ever-expanding,
                                    ever-receding,
                                    ever-escaping our vision
                                    but not depleting;
                                    only aging out
                                    of a life frequency
                                    that by its nature
                                    is transient and needing
                                    a sentient rest stop,
                                    on a universal road trip,
                                    from beginning
                                    to new beginnings.

They say that
the oldest light in the universe
contains coded information.

How many times
have I looked up
at darkened skies,
only to have my eyes
adjust and visit those
lonely, low-lit places;
and take the time
to learn the lessons,
from the only teachers
in a universe
of ever-aging light?

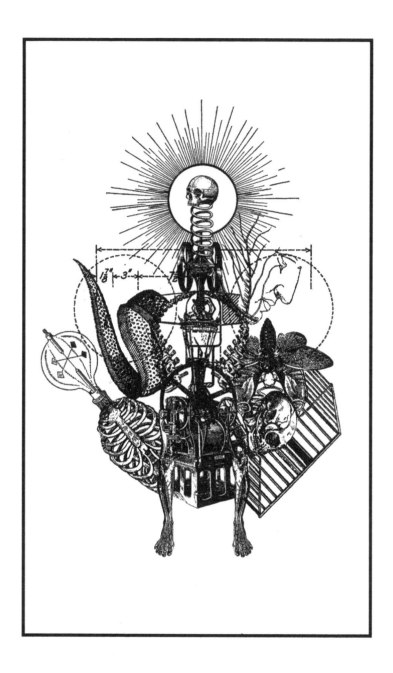

ACKNOWLEDGMENTS

Recalling all the people, places, and circumstances that inspired me while writing this book is impossible. However, I would be remiss if I did not at least try to remember—so let me try!

Melinda Ciaccio: my one and only constant. Mitch Green and Rad Press Publishing: my vision's partner. Phillip Kennedy Johnson, who told me to put down the chainsaw and pick up the chisel. Mia Bencivenga for her ninja editing prowess and back cover bad-assery. Kinsey Roehm for documenting several parts of this project through permanent dermal muraling. Every single guest on HACK sessions podcast: you are all my friends AND teachers. My four stellar colleagues of feedback: Samuel H. Hurley, for encouraging me to be "bold and glistening"; Joel Klenke, for being the best "intellectual fraud" to ever read my work; Susan Mulder, for her wise perspective from another artist's life; and Nick Hodges, for giving me his feedback in musical form, as well as coining a line that gave me four poems. Keenan McCarter, for my bio pic and favorite photo of myself (it's not because I don't want to show my face, its just a damn good picture!). Alanna Boudreau, whose casual eloquence in any given Instagram post of hers was unknowingly a significant influence of style, sound, and sense for me. Jodi and Keith Peters and the Peace of Grace Estate: a fitting retreat for my restless soul. To other "certain half-deserted streets" in my neighborhood, that were my "muttering retreats" for restless leg syndrome and mumbling poetry both to myself and the passing trees. Joe Rogan, Young Jaime, and the The Joe Rogan Experience Podcast. Your conversations with these people inspired much of this book: Whitney Cummings, Anthony Jeselnik, Tom Segura, Richard Dawkins, Russel Brand, and every damn episode with Duncan Trussell. But most especially: Chuck Palahniuk (#1158), for inspiring the poet out of me, Naval Ravikant (#1309), for so many wise seeds that sprouted many a poem in this book as well as others, and lastly (but not "leastly"), Brian Cox (#1233), who coined the first line of the first poem I wrote for this book—the titular poem at the end—with his contagious awe of the universe.

CPSIA information can be obtained
at www.ICGtesting.com
Printed in the USA
LVHW071529070821
694808LV00019B/529